IMAGES
of America

SHOWGIRLS OF LAS VEGAS

On the Cover: In this c. 1962 image, showgirls perform on the Stardust stage in a Donn Arden production of *Lido de Paris*. The *Lido* show, imported directly from Paris, France, debuted at the Stardust in July 1958 and ended its run in 1991, dimming the lights after more than three decades on the Las Vegas Strip. (Courtesy of University of Nevada, Las Vegas Special Collections.)

IMAGES
of America

SHOWGIRLS OF LAS VEGAS

Lisa Gioia-Acres

ARCADIA
PUBLISHING

ISBN 978-0-7385-9653-2

Published by Arcadia Publishing
Charleston, South Carolina

Printed in the United States of America

Library of Congress Control Number: 2012955599

For all general information, please contact Arcadia Publishing:
Telephone 843-853-2070
Fax 843-853-0044
E-mail sales@arcadiapublishing.com
For customer service and orders:
Toll-Free 1-888-313-2665

Visit us on the Internet at www.arcadiapublishing.com

To the many wonderful people I have met in Las Vegas who offered encouragement, love, and a willingness to share their stories

Contents

Foreword

As a little girl, I grew up dancing along with the June Taylor Dancers on Jackie Gleason specials on the television. After years of dance training, I auditioned for shows that took me all over the world. I came to Las Vegas and found my calling as a showgirl in several productions before landing my dream spot on the *Lido de Paris* stage at the Stardust, joining a cast of 60 that even included an elephant! The cast and crew became my second family and still are to this day. I hold my memories of that time dear to my heart. As someone who realized her dreams on the Las Vegas stage, I am proud to help introduce the world to the beautiful Las Vegas showgirl.

—Suzan Hiett Rawlings
Las Vegas showgirl for 30 years

ACKNOWLEDGMENTS

While conducting research for this book, I had the privilege to meet so many wonderful individuals who opened their scrapbooks and shared their stories with me. Longtime friends and Las Vegas treasures Bo Boisvert, Milt Bozanic, Carey Burke, Ed Dodrill, Phil Jensen, and Frank Valeri shared their personal photographic collections with me and added a unique flavor to this book. A debt of gratitude belongs to former showgirls Doll-E Eaglin, Rusty Feuer, Suzan Hiett Rawlings, Ingrid Jackson, Virginia James, Stacy Law, LaVerne Ligon, and Mistinguett. Their generosity and encouragement made this journey memorable for me. When my daughter asked me if I secretly wanted to be a showgirl, I can honestly say that after meeting these amazing women, the answer is "yes." I would like to thank Su Kim Chung, Kelli Luchs, Peter Michel, Sara Miller, Joyce Moore, and Claytee White for their help and words of encouragement. The staff members at both the Nevada State Museum, Las Vegas, and the University of Nevada, Las Vegas, generously allowed me access to their collections.

The University of Nevada, Las Vegas (UNLV) houses unique, rare, and specialized research material that documents the history, culture, and physical environment of the city of Las Vegas, the Southern Nevada region, the gaming industry, and the university itself. The UNLV collections include books, pamphlets, posters, serials and periodicals, scrapbooks, archives and manuscripts, maps, architectural drawings, photographs, and video and audio recordings.

Introduction

Las Vegas is known the world over, whether as a gambling mecca or for its former mob connections, Howard Hughes, the Rat Pack, as a town that never sleeps, as "Sin City," or for the infamous marketing catchphrase "what happens in Vegas stays in Vegas." Some of the city's lesser-known treasures include the area's outdoor adventure opportunities, its Native American heritage, the soon-to-be-realized Ice Age Park, the dedication of community service organizations, and—last but not least—showgirls.

The Las Vegas showgirl is a lasting beacon connecting the Las Vegas of the past to the Las Vegas of today. Unlike many of the historic hotels/casinos that have met with a wrecking ball, the showgirl endures.

The El Rancho Vegas, which opened in April 1941, was the first casino on the Las Vegas Strip to employ dancing girls whose purpose was to provide a diversion for the audience between acts. These proto-showgirls spent mere minutes on stage, and with contracts lasting only two weeks, they appeared to be a novelty. But from these humble beginnings at a small Las Vegas hotel, the dancing girls evolved to become the iconic showgirls parading and prancing across every major and minor property along the Strip. Every hotel vied to outdo the other, creating high-budget, over-the-top productions with showgirls as the centerpiece. These included the Copa Girls at the Sands, the Moro-Landis dancers at the Sahara, the Rangerettes at the Riviera, and the Jimmy Durante Girls at the Desert Inn, to name just a few. In the late 1940s, dancing girls took to the stage for the first time, and by the 1950s and 1960s, showgirls had arrived.

Visionary showmen like Jack Entratter, Donn Arden, Lou Walters, and Frederic Apcar upped the ante every time they conceived of a new theme to impress the multitudes that crowded Las Vegas showrooms and lounges. Utilizing the creative talents of costume designers and choreographers, these men brought the glitz and glamour of Paris and Hollywood to the desert.

The show would certainly not have gone on without the people behind the scenes: those who sewed the costumes and dressed the dancers, those who constructed the sets and ensured they could withstand thousands of performances, the company managers who practiced tough love on their overworked charges, and the girls who showed up six days a week and performed two shows a night wearing smiles that outshined the brightest neon marquee.

The showgirl's life was a grueling one, with hazards, injuries, and insults as common as the "oohs" and "ahhs" that made it all worthwhile. They were outfitted in beautiful clothes created by the world's most sought-after designers but worried over every step taken and every pound gained. They experienced adoration from afar but had to sidestep groping from patrons who assumed that showgirls were as accessible as the cheap food and slot machines. They faced brutal competition waiting in the wings, as the life of a showgirl appeared to be a glamorous stepping-stone to greater opportunities. The women came in droves to auditions and showed up for work despite sore feet, strep throat, sick kids, and demanding bosses; they knew their lives were privileged, and they carried their roles as Las Vegas ambassadors with pride and grace.

The big productions featuring headliners and showgirls have given way to other shows, like Cirque du Soleil, and to clubs that push the morality envelope in ways that would make a topless revue dancer blush. Only one holdout remains—*Jubilee!* at Bally's, a show that has been running for over 30 years with no end in sight. Showgirls can still be seen making the rounds on the arm of former Las Vegas mayor Oscar Goodman and outside of myriad casinos posing for photographs with tourists, but these are mere facsimiles of the elusive, untouchable, alluring showgirl of yesteryear. Like the voices of Frank Sinatra and Dean Martin, the era of the Las Vegas showgirl has faded into obscurity. Within the pages of this book, however, showgirls continue to live on through the images and stories of how they made Las Vegas the entertainment capital of the world.

One

The Showgirl Arrives

A Las Vegas showgirl exudes beauty, elicits fantasy, and is placed upon a pedestal both literally and figuratively. Before a hopeful can achieve this status, she must go through a grueling process of auditioning and face the possibility of rejection. If chosen, however, her life becomes a whirlwind of rehearsals, challenging dance moves in cumbersome yet exquisitely designed costumes, and outrageous offers from admirers. (Courtesy of Bo Boisvert.)

A casting call for Las Vegas showgirls lures hundreds of women, each one hoping to stand out among the crowd. Housewives, secretaries, models, and classical dancers were among the eclectic group of women vying for a place in a Las Vegas extravaganza. (Courtesy of UNLV Special Collections.)

The men review potential showgirls, and the women stand rigidly as spotlights beam down on them. (Courtesy of UNLV Special Collections.)

Jack Entratter (seated second from right), known as the "Sagebrush Showman," participates in the interview process. A veteran of East Coast nightclubs, most notably the Copacabana in New York City, he became the entertainment director for the Sands and set out in search of the "most beautiful girls in the west." (Courtesy of UNLV Special Collections.)

Women who appear nonchalant and a man with a poker face scrutinize showgirl hopefuls, possibly for a spot in a show or for an upcoming contest. (Courtesy of UNLV Special Collections.)

HIWAY 91 — LAS VEGAS, NEVADA — DUdley 2-7100

January 16-17/1959

COPAGIRL APPLICATION

Name____________________ Age________

Address____________________ Phone________

City____________ Zone____ State________

Height____ ft____ inches Weight______ lbs.

Hair Color______ Eyes Color______ Complexion______

Bust Measurement______ Waist______ Hips______

Dress Size______ Bathing Suit Size____ Hat____ Shoes____

Present Occupation____________________

Ambition____________________

Why did you apply for a Copagirl position?____________

____

a place in the sun

LOS ANGELES OFFICE: 9508 WILSHIRE BLVD., BEVERLY HILLS — TELEPHONE BRADSHAW 2-8611
NEW YORK OFFICE: 48 WEST 48th STREET, N. Y. 36, N. Y. — TELEPHONE PLAZA 7-4454

An application to become a Copa Girl asks for information such as body measurements and shoe size. One hopeful, answering the prompt about why she applied for a Copa Girl position, wrote, "Excitement and glamour." (Courtesy of UNLV Special Collections.)

Sands Copa Girls were young women who, according to Jack Entratter, need only be pretty and pleasing. Entratter once said, "I don't care if they never dance. They're beautiful and I want beauty." (Courtesy of UNLV Special Collections.)

A much-hyped media promotion to find Copa Girls resulted in a new crop of handpicked beauties from all over Texas. Here, they pose for a promotional photograph with a flag of Texas upon their arrival in Las Vegas. (Courtesy of UNLV Special Collections.)

Sands entertainment director and show producer Jack Entratter had a specific size in mind when casting his showgirls. They were to weigh around 116 pounds and be approximately five feet and four inches tall. Their overall measurements were to be: 32-to-34-inch bust, 24-inch waist, and 34-inch hips. (Courtesy of UNLV Special Collections.)

Virginia James, a Copa Girl who hailed from El Paso, Texas, personified Entratter's classic beauty with her small-featured, American-girl looks. James helped open the Sands in the early 1950s. (Courtesy of UNLV Special Collections.)

The Las Vegas showgirl did not arrive on the scene until the 1950s. Before that time, chorus or dancing girls provided an amusing distraction for audience members between acts. Here, a dancer performs a high kick for producer Harold Minsky (far right, with pipe) for one of his early burlesque shows. (Courtesy of UNLV Special Collections.)

Although topless showgirls did not appear on stage until the late 1950s, when Harold Minsky introduced the idea to the town of Las Vegas, a practically perfect female body was always a requirement to perform. Auditioning women had to forgo modesty and subject their bodies to scrutiny. No surgical scars, tattoos, or tan lines were allowed. (Courtesy of UNLV Special Collections.)

In addition to having perfect skin, a showgirl had to be in top form in order to withstand the weight of costumes while performing complicated dance moves. Some producers, such as Donn Arden, only hired trained dancers for their shows. (Courtesy of UNLV Special Collections.)

In this 1954 image, Ziegfeld Follies choreographer Bob Gilbert watches a dancer during a dress rehearsal in the Sands Copa Room. (Courtesy of UNLV Special Collections.)

Here, the Bluebell Girls arrive at the Las Vegas airport after a trip from Paris, France. They are accompanied by Margaret Kelly (fourth from left), known as "Madame Bluebell." A classically trained dancer who performed with Maurice Chevalier and Josephine Baker, Kelly met Donn Arden in Europe, and together they brought *Lido de Paris* to Las Vegas. *Lido* was to be a true import for its entire run: the girls, costumes, sets, and choreography all originated in Paris. (Courtesy of UNLV Special Collections.)

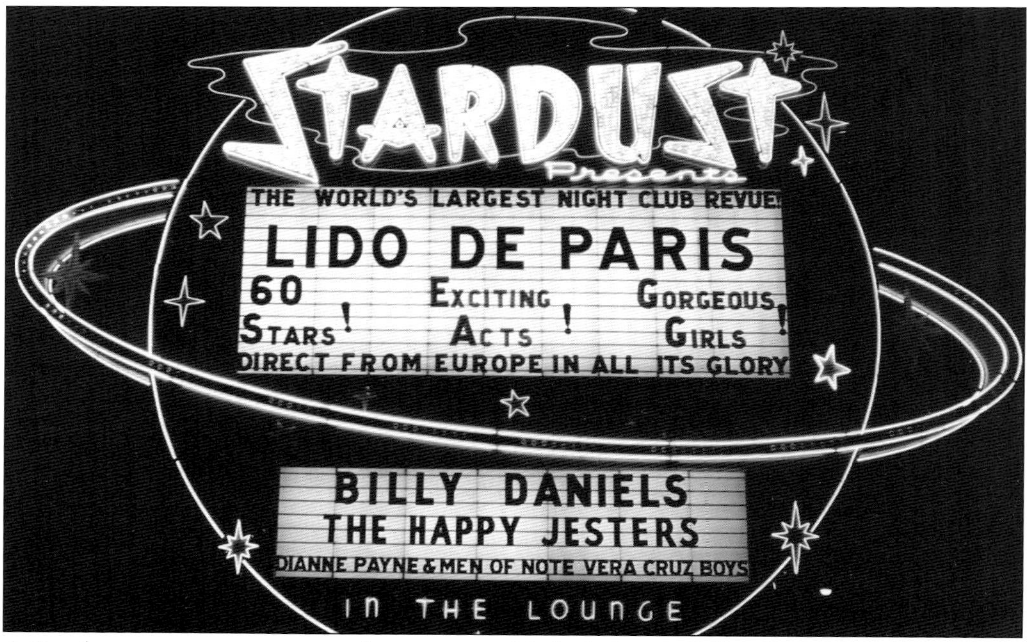

A Stardust marquee announces the opening of *Lido de Paris*, produced and choreographed by Donn Arden. (Courtesy of Frank Valeri.)

The era of the Las Vegas show extravaganza arrived when principal owner Jake Freedman and general manager Jack Entratter opened the Sands on December 15, 1952, with a show featuring star Danny Thomas (pictured above with the Copa Girls). The total cost of the costumes worn by the dancers exceeded $12,000—more than what Thomas was paid as the show's headlining act. (Courtesy of Virginia James.)

Celebrities and showgirls became mainstays of Las Vegas entertainment. In this image from March 1957, Dean Martin rehearses a number at the Sands. (Courtesy of UNLV Special Collections.)

In addition to performing on stage, showgirls vied for the "Showgirl of the Year" title. Here, a winner kisses Sands producer and general manager Jack Entratter. (Courtesy of UNLV Special Collections.)

Being a showgirl could open doors to other opportunities. Several showgirls went on to perform in Hollywood movies or to dance on stages around the world. Valerie Perrine (pictured at right), who was nominated for an Academy Award for best actress, got her start as a showgirl for the Stardust in the 1960s. Other former showgirls who went on to appear in Hollywood include Bek Nelson, June Allyson, and Lucille Bremer. (Courtesy of UNLV Special Collections.)

Ffolliott Charlton performs in one of the early shows featuring dancers at the El Rancho Vegas. Charlton started her career as a dancer but eventually became Donn Arden's right-hand woman, changing her name to Fluff LeCoque. As company manager for Arden's *Hallelujah Hollywood* and *Jubilee!*, she ensured the shows went off without a hitch. (Courtesy of UNLV Special Collections.)

Florenz Ziegfeld, who produced the first "Follies" in 1907, is the inspiration for Jack Entratter's image of the perfect woman. Ziegfeld became known as the "glorifier" for his excellent eye for feminine beauty. Las Vegas showgirls came to be the epitome of perfection. In the photograph below, a showgirl models a fur coat for an audience of admiring women. (Courtesy of UNLV Special Collections.)

Showgirls crowd together in a dressing room in what appear to be Oriental-themed costumes. The woman in the central background is a dresser; she is helping one of the girls into her costume. (Courtesy of Virginia James.)

The Las Vegas showgirl was becoming known the world over, as evidenced by the cover story in this June 21, 1954, edition of *Life* magazine. (Courtesy of UNLV Special Collections.)

In this 1954 photograph, showgirls check to see if they "measure up" to the standard. Jack Entratter liked his girls to be under five feet and five inches tall, while Donn Arden insisted on his dancers being five feet and eight inches or taller. (Courtesy of UNLV Special Collections.)

Costumed showgirls sit in a dressing room on a break from performing. This historic photograph was taken at the Moulin Rouge, the first integrated casino and hotel in Las Vegas. After opening in May 1955, the Moulin Rouge welcomed both black and white entertainers and patrons, providing stiff competition to Strip properties with policies that excluded blacks from amenities and services outside of the stage on which they performed. (Courtesy of UNLV Special Collections.)

In the 1955 image at left, Copa Girl Linda Lawson is crowned "Miss-Cue" while surrounded by military personnel. The era of atomic testing was a boon for Las Vegas, and, naturally, the showgirl's potential for getting nationwide attention was utilized. Miss-Cue was named after a failed atomic test initially called Operation Cue but redubbed "Operation Miscue" after high winds caused delays in its deployment. (Courtesy of UNLV Special Collections.)

As demonstrated in this c. 1958 photograph, Jerry Lewis cannot help but yuck it up with dancers during a rehearsal. A close look reveals the taped marks on the floor, which provided a guide for dancers getting into position. The empty orchestra pit is visible in the background. (Courtesy of UNLV Special Collections.)

The opening of a casino often required a big blast to draw the attention of the media. As a promotional hook, the Stardust placed showgirls atop this larger-than-life firecracker. (Courtesy of Frank Valeri.)

Dunes showgirls put a different spin on the 1950s trend that involved college students jamming as many of themselves as possible into telephone booths. (Courtesy of Bo Boisvert.)

In between and after shows, many showgirls were required to "dress up the joint," which meant hanging out in the casino while mingling with patrons. Here, showgirls offer luck to gamblers at a craps table. Girls under 21 were not allowed in the casinos, so they waited in dressing rooms under the protective eyes of stage and company managers until showtime. (Courtesy of UNLV Special Collections.)

Always on hand to help promote their city, showgirls were often the main attraction during the Helldorado Days festival. In the photograph at left, Bluebell dancers from the Stardust ride through downtown Las Vegas waving to admirers from their company's float. The Pioneer Club sign is visible in the background. (Courtesy of UNLV Special Collections.)

In this May 1955 image, showgirls from the Moulin Rouge play around in the kitchen, fitting perfectly into large cooking pots. (Courtesy of UNLV Special Collections.)

At right, an unidentified Copa Girl and choreographer Bob Gilbert pose outside of the Sands Hotel. (Courtesy of UNLV Special Collections.)

Handsome opera singer Robert Merrill poses with a showgirl while fellow cast members peek around the corner in the background. Notice how the showgirl adjusts her stance in order to not tower over the star. (Courtesy of Bo Boisvert.)

Another Las Vegas headliner, comedian and television personality Sam Levenson, is surrounded by showgirls as he stands out against their backdrop of white feathers. (Courtesy of Bo Boisvert.)

“Cheesecake” photographs like this were used to advertise Las Vegas and all it had to offer. (Courtesy of Milt Bozanic.)

Showgirls wave from atop a Flamingo hotel diving board, inviting visitors to Las Vegas for fun in the sun. (Courtesy of UNLV Special Collections.)

Sunglasses-clad showgirls create a living Christmas tree, complete with presents, a reindeer, bells, and tinsel. (Courtesy of UNLV Special Collections.)

These showgirls are decorating a Joshua tree—a plant found in abundance in the Mojave Desert—for Christmas. (Courtesy of UNLV Special Collections.)

In this promotional photograph, showgirls surround a larger-than-life cake replica of The Mint. (Courtesy of UNLV Special Collections.)

Mickey Rooney transports showgirls on a rickshaw during a stint headlining at the Riviera Hotel and Casino. (Courtesy of UNLV Special Collections.)

Showgirls surround Sands co-owner and Houston businessman Jake Freedman as they pose for a publicity photograph at the Las Vegas airport. Freedman arrived in Las Vegas in 1952 and, together with Jack Entratter, ushered in the era of high-end entertainment on the Strip. Freedman died in 1958 at the age of 64. (Courtesy of Bo Boisvert.)

Jack Entratter and an unidentified showgirl talk to two enthralled girls on stage in the Copa Room at the Sands. (Courtesy of UNLV Special Collections.)

Las Vegas showgirl costumes were showcased in a paper-doll book called *Showgirls of Las Vegas: Cut-Out Paper Dolls*, which contained 10 different outfits. The "Gay Paree" costume pictured at left is adorned with purple feathers, a strategically placed jeweled necklace, fishnet stockings, and a plumed headdress. (Courtesy of UNLV Special Collections.)

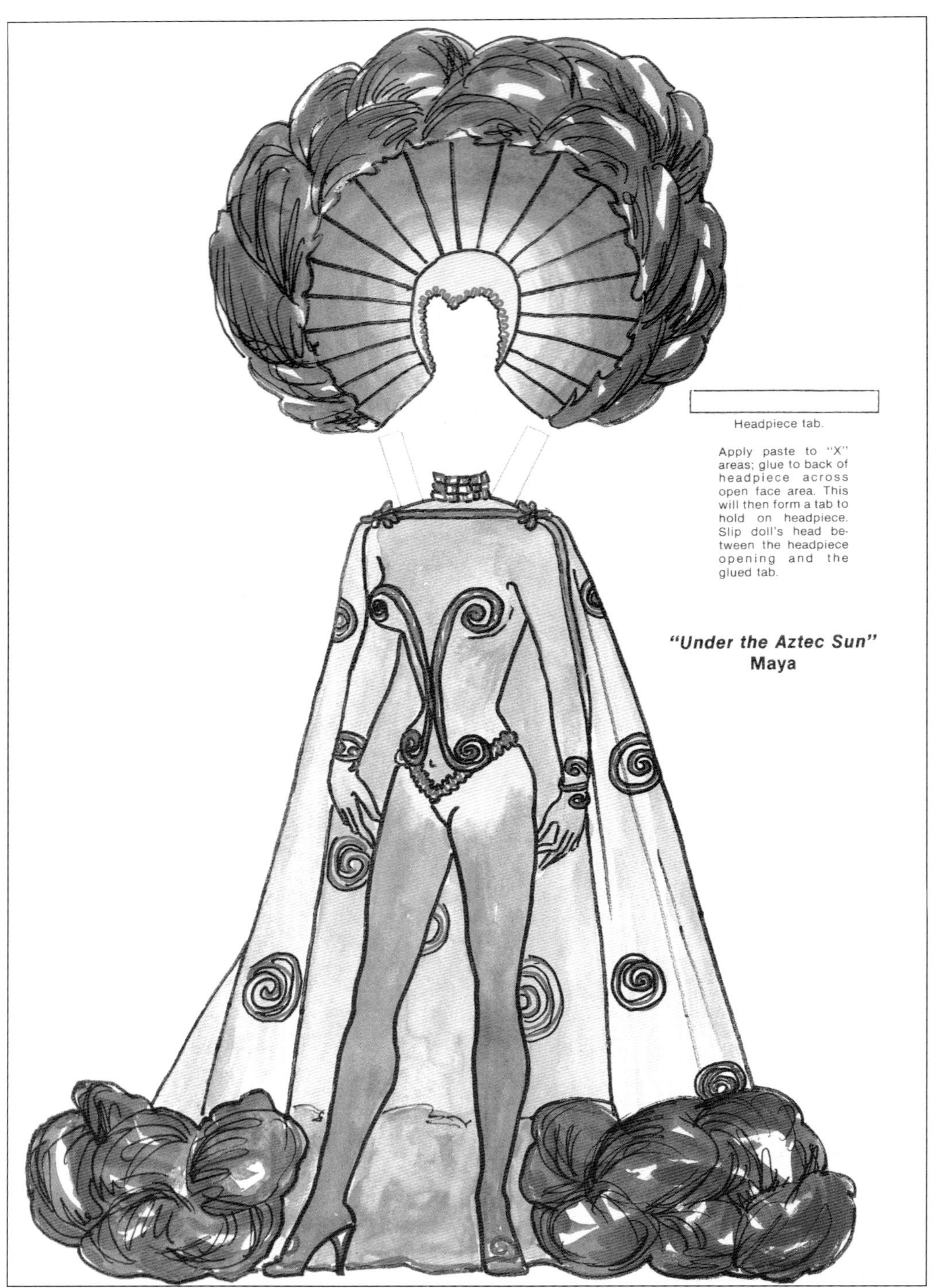

This Aztec Goddess costume is resplendent in the colors of the sun—red and gold. This image (as well as the one on the bottom of page 33) comes from a rare book found in the University of Nevada, Las Vegas Special Collections library archives. (Courtesy of UNLV Special Collections.)

It was an art form to design costumes for Las Vegas showgirls. Designers such as Ray Aghayan, Bob Mackie, Pete Menefee, and José Luis Viñas (whose design is shown at right) were perfectionists. The shows were often built around a designer's creations, with choreography developed to showcase the costumes rather than the music or the showgirls. (Courtesy of UNLV Special Collections.)

This sketch shows a José Luis Viñas costume designed to clothe a nude (topless only) showgirl. The costume includes draped rhinestones and feathers. (Courtesy of UNLV Special Collections.)

The stills from this unidentified film shot in the 1950s or 1960s might have been used as a commercial or by a casino for some other promotional endeavor. An actor portrays a lost miner dying in the desert who is rescued by showgirls, who shield the unconscious man from the brutal desert sun using their feathered fans. Modern advertising campaigns still use showgirls to promote Las Vegas. (Both courtesy of UNLV Special Collections.)

In an effort to consistently surprise the audience, choreographers became quite inventive. Here, showgirl Theresa Hayes balances on a ball. Also pictured are, from left to right, unidentified, Margo Martin, Dean Martin (no relation to Margo), Pat Hewlett, Sands general manager Jack Entratter, and Lucille Nelson. (Courtesy of UNLV Special Collections.)

In this 1954 image, Frank Sinatra stands at far left while Jack Entratter and his choreographer and stage manager discuss a dress rehearsal. Conflicts often arise during rehearsals. If a costume is unmanageable, wardrobe people have to scramble to make adjustments, sometimes finishing at the last moment before a showgirl struts onto the stage. (Courtesy of UNLV Special Collections.)

In this 1960s photograph, Frank Sinatra (left) and Dean Martin sing a number along with a backup chorus of showgirls at the Sands. The showgirl's role was not limited to dancing and parading across the stage; quite often, they also had to have a talent for singing as well. (Courtesy of UNLV Special Collections.)

Comedian Tommy "Moe" Raft, who performed in Minsky's Burlesque in the 1970s, mugs for the camera, seemingly disconcerted by such a bevy of beautiful showgirls. (Courtesy of UNLV Special Collections.)

Jack Entratter (left) and Wally Cox admire a group of showgirls. This picture may have been taken when they were judges for a Showgirl of the Year contest. (Courtesy of UNLV Special Collections.)

Jerry Lewis (left) and Dean Martin mimic the leg lifts of showgirls who were set to perform with them in an upcoming number. (Courtesy of UNLV Special Collections.)

Showgirls help Sammy Davis Jr. (center) and an unidentified woman celebrate the birthday of American actor William Bendix (pictured to the right of Davis). (Courtesy of Bo Boisvert.)

This rehearsal photograph shows a "Tiller line," which many Americans associate with the Radio City Music Hall's Rockettes. It consists of precision dancers who are able to execute kicks in sync; this takes considerable concentration and talent. (Courtesy of UNLV Special Collections.)

Show producer Donn Arden is not afraid to "show them how it's done." In this 1970s photograph, Arden dances alongside his cast in order to illustrate his vision for a number. (Courtesy of UNLV Special Collections.)

Two

It's Showtime

In the 1950s, over-the-top shows produced by the most recognized names in show business opened on the Las Vegas Strip. This 1958 photograph was taken during the first performance of *C'est Magnifique*, the first edition of Donn Arden's *Lido de Paris*. (Courtesy of UNLV Special Collections.)

The Dunes Hotel and Country Club opened its doors in 1955. In 1961, producer and director Frederic Apcar brought his French influence to the Strip with *Vive les Girls*, a small, intimate lounge show. He then presented *Casino de Paris*—with a cast of 100—in a larger, main-room venue. This 1978 photograph shows performers dressed in Marie Antoinette–era costumes during a number from *Casino de Paris*. (Courtesy of UNLV Special Collections.)

This promotional poster is for the Dunes Hotel and Country Club and its Frederic Apcar–produced show, *Casino de Paris*. (Courtesy of UNLV Special Collections.)

Hollywood star Rhonda Fleming made her singing debut at the newly opened Tropicana Hotel on May 20, 1957. Wearing a "nude" gown designed by Don Loper and backed by the Tropicana Girls, Fleming wowed audiences and critics alike. *Los Angeles Herald-Express* columnist Jimmy Starr expressed it best: "The atomic bomb didn't explode last night, but a new and lovely nightclub star—Rhonda Fleming—blasted her way at the Tropicana and made pretty music that was strictly big time stuff." (Courtesy of Bo Boisvert.)

Audience members get an up close and personal view of performers. This number is one of many produced and choreographed by Donn Arden in *Lido de Paris*. (Courtesy of UNLV Special Collections.)

The El Rancho Vegas, the first casino on the Strip, opened in 1941 and offered entertainment in the Round-Up Room (later called the Opera House). Chorus line dancers the El Rancho Girls shared the stage with singers, comedians, and a headliner. According to dancer Nancy Williams, the stage was so small that only eight girls could fit on it—"one more and a dancer would fall off the stage!" (Courtesy of Nancy Williams.)

El Rancho Vegas
Queen
OF THE
WEST

"EMBODYING TO THE FULLEST
THE CHARM AND ROMANTIC
ALLURE OF THE
WESTERN WONDERLAND"

A Sportsman's Paradise

This is an original program for the El Rancho Vegas. The newly opened resort promoted itself as the "Queen of the West" and as a "Sportsman's Paradise." (Courtesy of Nancy Williams.)

Showgirls appear in costume for the Arabian Nights performance of *Minsky's Follies* at the Dunes in the 1960s. The Dunes opened in May 1955 but closed soon after due to financial problems. It reopened again in 1956 and enjoyed success until its closing and ultimate demolition in 1993. (Courtesy of UNLV Special Collections.)

Las Vegas is known for pushing the envelope, which has its roots in the 1950s when Harold Minsky brought his topless burlesque show to town, spurring an uproar from citizenry and religious leaders alike. The practice is still alive and well today, with exposed breasts, as one showgirl comments, taking their place on stage in a "supporting role." (Courtesy of UNLV Special Collections.)

A battle raged over the nude showgirls. In this September 7, 1958, article from the *Las Vegas Review-Journal*, topless dancers from the El Rancho Vegas are featured alongside showgirls from the Sands, the one Strip property that promised to "never go nude," prompting a deluge of supportive letters from community members, tourists, and even the local Catholic diocese. (Courtesy of UNLV Special Collections.)

SUNDAY NEWS, SEPTEMBER 7, 1958 C9

Las Vegas' Nude Look

Battle of the Bosoms Bares All

Some Las Vegas show girls are showing more and more these days in the War of the Nudes which is raging there. Barry Ashton, choreographer at El Rancho Vegas, has covered up his girls somewhat (←), but we had to cover 'em even more. These chorines (▲) are swathed in clothes at The Sands, an anti-nudity outpost.

A dancing poodle plays second fiddle to star performer Phil Harris and costumed showgirls. Animals were often involved in Las Vegas productions. (Courtesy of Rusty Taylor Feuer.)

Some show animals posed little danger to the performers or the audience. Here, a "gorilla" is part of *Vive les Girls* in the Dunes lounge, creating yet another Las Vegas illusion. (Courtesy of UNLV Special Collections.)

Casino de Paris, imported from Paris, France, opened at the Dunes in 1963. This 1978 image captures performing showgirls and show boys. (Courtesy of UNLV Special Collections.)

Casino de Paris and *Vive les Girls* choreographer Ron Lewis incorporated an African theme in many of his dance numbers. At right, showgirl Peggy Kubena poses next to Caesar the lion, another animal that helped put Las Vegas show productions over the top. (Courtesy of UNLV Special Collections.)

Barely-there costumes are offset by large, plumed headdresses. Principal dancers are showcased front and center on stage, setting them apart from the rest of the cast. Principal dancers had their names highlighted in bold in the program and enjoyed higher salaries, their own dressing rooms, and the best costumes and lighting. (Courtesy of UNLV Special Collections.)

Bluebells, the dancers in Donn Arden shows at the Stardust, are accompanied by a male dancer whose high kick matches their own. This 1958 image shows a number from *C'est Magnifique*, the first edition of the *Lido de Paris* show. (Courtesy of UNLV Special Collections.)

The New Frontier was one of the many Strip properties to showcase "family burlesque" productions created by Harold Minsky. Nearly-nude showgirls were considered a flash in the pan.

The Thunderbird Hotel opened on Labor Day in 1948. This photograph shows the hotel marquee announcing the show *Thoroughly Modern Minsky*, a 1960s production. In August 1959, the Thunderbird presented the first partially-nude ice show, *Ecstasy on Ice*. One of the catchphrases used to promote the hotel and casino was, "Remember, you saw it at the Thunderbird first."

This Sands marquee announces the appearance of Nat King Cole on January 14, 1960, along with the Copa Girls. Like all black entertainers of the era, Cole was allowed to perform in Strip properties, but once the show was over, he had to find food and lodging elsewhere. (Courtesy of UNLV Special Collections.)

Segregation meant little behind the scenes, as demonstrated in this photograph of Copa Girls helping Nat "The King" Cole celebrate his birthday. (Courtesy of Virginia James.)

Black entertainers found willing integrated audiences at the Moulin Rouge Hotel, an off-Strip property. The hotel, which opened on May 24, 1955, was touted as the nation's first interracial hotel. The Moulin Rouge experienced an early demise when it closed just six months later. (Courtesy of UNLV Special Collections.)

The marquee of the Stardust show, *Lido de Paris*, stands out against a background filled with other Strip resorts that had begun to dot the Las Vegas landscape. (Courtesy of Frank Valeri.)

At the south end of Las Vegas Boulevard sits the Tropicana, enticing travelers from Southern California to go no further for their entertainment. The *Folies Bergere* first came to the hotel in 1959, when entertainment director Lou Walters (father of journalist Barbara Walters) secured the rights to bring the Paris extravaganza to Las Vegas. (Courtesy of LaVerne Ligon and Leonard Polk.)

By the 1970s, Las Vegas had progressed. In 1974, Donn Arden opened *Hallelujah Hollywood*, a production that celebrated Hollywood musicals, at the MGM Grand. For the first time, black showgirls and dancers performed on a stage on the Las Vegas Strip. (Courtesy of LaVerne Ligon and Leonard Polk.)

This photograph shows *Hallelujah Hollywood*'s Living Curtain. Showgirls, referred to as the Cat Pack in this production, descend to the stage from a series of five-by-four-foot platforms and stairs, performing a choreographed number between pauses. The Living Curtain was used in several productions in different venues along the Strip. Dancers stepped carefully and had no railing to hold on to as they descended the stairs in a dark theater. Some (but not all) properties offered hazard pay to dancers performing this risky number. (Courtesy of LaVerne Ligon and Leonard Polk.)

Once all of the dancers had arrived on stage, a female singer would appear dressed as the "Ringmaster." The MGM logo centered in the Curtain would rotate, revealing "Leo the Lion," who—depending on whether he was feeling up to it—might roar loudly to the delight of the crowd. (Courtesy of UNLV Special Collections.)

Showgirls perch on "sky disks," platforms suspended from the ceiling that added a unique dimension to the spectator's experience. (Courtesy of UNLV Special Collections.)

This example of an elaborate stage setup is complete with sky disks, a staircase, and glittering chandeliers. Showgirls, some of whom perform topless, are bedecked in lavish costumes. The principal dancer is on the raised platform accompanied by male dancers. This scene is from a 1970s or 1980s finale of the MGM Grand production *Hallelujah Hollywood*. (Courtesy of UNLV Special Collections.)

Audience members at *Lido de Paris* gaze upward at showgirls on trapeze swings. Many showgirls put years of dance training to good use when choreographers, always looking to astonish the crowd, created new numbers. (Courtesy of UNLV Special Collections.)

Circus performers ride unicycles while a showgirl poses at the Circus Circus Hotel and Casino. (Courtesy of UNLV Special Collections.)

A feathered showgirl parades among the audience upon the catwalk, or *pasarela*, giving the audience a closer look at the stunning attire worn by a principal dancer. Behind her are showgirls, some of whom are topless. Ingrid Jackson, a showgirl in the MGM Grand production *Hallelujah Hollywood*, recalled hearing females in the audience try to distract their male escorts from looking at the bare-breasted women by pointing out other interesting aspects of the show, such as "Look at that set!" (Courtesy of UNLV Special Collections.)

One showgirl walked the *pasarela* just weeks after giving birth; when her breast milk began unexpectedly leaking, she used her feathered boa to cover herself. This is but one example of the real-life trials faced by women in pursuit of a career in the showgirl business. (Courtesy of UNLV Special Collections.)

Harold Minsky (right) examines part of a costume while chatting with show manager Eddie Lynch. Fur from foxes, chinchilla, and mink were often used in early showgirl costumes. (Courtesy of UNLV Special Collections.)

In addition to fur muffs, hats, and collars, costumes in this number were made of plush velvet. Each showgirl in this photograph, taken at the Thunderbird Hotel and Casino, looks unique. In future productions, as the "showgirl" persona became more defined, performers began to look alike and hair was often hidden under elaborate headdresses. Showgirls came to be seen by some as "mannequins"—props to show off costumes and sets. (Courtesy of Nancy Williams.)

José Luis Viñas, a designer from Spain, created costumes for the Dunes shows *Casino de Paris* and *Viva les Girls*. This sketch by Viñas shows both costume and set designs. (Courtesy of UNLV Special Collections.)

The Viñas sketch comes to life in this number. Showgirls draped in towel headdresses perform while seated in bathtubs filled with water and illuminated by a mirrored backdrop. (Courtesy of UNLV Special Collections.)

Bluebell Valda Boyne gets her costume fitted by head wardrobe mistress Emily Warren while costume designer Louis Folco looks on. Early showgirl costumes were created with a much simpler cut and contained no feathers, boas, or ruffles. Costumes were custom-made for each performer right down to the shoes, which were made to fit by tracing the girl's foot on cardboard during the design process. (Courtesy of UNLV Special Collections.)

The wardrobe people were the backbone of every production. According to Gale Baker, author of *Neon Queens*, there would be five dressers for every 20 dancers, with each costume made to perfectly fit the dancer's body. In the number shown below, there are numerous costume designs and materials, and some of the dancers are holding lighted candelabras. (Courtesy of Bo Boisvert.)

Wearing outrageous headdresses like those pictured above made it awkward and even dangerous for showgirls to descend stairs. Counting was the only way to know when the stage would appear underfoot. Woe to the woman whose mind wandered as she was descending; one misstep could mean a tumble onto the stage. (Courtesy of UNLV Special Collections.)

The Desert Inn was home to *Pzazz*, a production with a cast of 100 that celebrated American culture from the 1930s to the 1960s. According to a promotional brochure, it took 110 seamstresses working 12 hours a day, six days a week, for five weeks to create the costumes for the lavish production numbers. Here, the cast, dressed in *Beau Geste* costumes, gathers for the show's first anniversary in 1968. (Courtesy of Rusty Taylor Feuer.)

This c. 1970 photograph captures the Grecian look featured on the set and in costumes worn by showgirls in "Blue and Beautiful," one of the strikingly choreographed numbers in *Pzazz*, which was produced by Donn Arden at the Desert Inn. (Courtesy of UNLV Special Collections.)

Another c. 1970 photograph features angels in the "Halo Hi-Jinx" number from *Pzazz*. The showgirls wear golden cupids atop mile-high headdresses, pink and white feathered wings, and bikini bottoms. (Courtesy of UNLV Special Collections.)

Flowered parasols are held aloft by dancing showgirls in this 1977 edition of the *Lido de Paris* at the Stardust. (Courtesy of UNLV Special Collections.)

Showgirls stay in step as they perform in costumes covered with feathers, boas, and rhinestones. (Courtesy of UNLV Special Collections.)

In this 1978 image, male dancers lift a showgirl high above the crowd in this Egyptian-themed number at the Dunes. (Courtesy of UNLV Special Collections.)

Showgirls from the Last Frontier wear ruffles and petticoats as three men perhaps toast their luck in being surrounded by so many beautiful women. (Courtesy of UNLV Special Collections.)

This photograph shows the entire cast of *Jubilee!* at the MGM Grand in 1980. On July 30, 2011, *Jubilee!* (now at Bally's) celebrated its 30th anniversary. It is the longest-running show on the Las

Vegas Strip. (Courtesy of UNLV Special Collections.)

Showgirls and show boys perform the Golden Galaxy number of Pzazz at the Stardust in 1970. Two of the dancers lounge on beds suspended from the ceiling. (Courtesy of UNLV Special Collections.)

A showgirl balances precariously on a letter in a production of Panache, another Donn Arden-produced show. (Courtesy of UNLV Special Collections.)

Donn Arden, surrounded by showgirls including Jackie Matthews, Diane Findley, Eileen Barnett, and Tricia Lee, cuts into a cake celebrating the opening of the 1970s production of *Hallelujah Hollywood* at the MGM Grand. (Courtesy of UNLV Special Collections.)

This is the cover of a program for the *Hallelujah Hollywood* show at the MGM Grand, which celebrated the world of Hollywood movies. (Courtesy of Ingrid Gates Jackson.)

Management and cast celebrate the closing show of the first *Lido de Paris* at the Stardust in the fall of 1959. Entertainment director Frank Sennes is seated in the front at left. Other men in the photograph include Allard Roen, Tom McDonald, Milton Jaffe, and Johnny Drew. (Courtesy of UNLV Special Collections.)

In this November 1963 image from the Sands Copa Room, singer Harry Nofal does a calypso number surrounded by showgirls, including one with an interesting playing-card headdress. A short railing separated the performers from the seated audience—a precautionary implement placed to help dancers gauge the distance to the edge of the stage. Rusty Taylor Feuer recalls several incidents when showgirls landed in the laps of audience members, one of many accidents that happened before management sought ways to make the stage safer for performers.

A technician watches a production in progress from behind the scenes. The performance is visible on his monitor. (Courtesy of UNLV Special Collections.)

In this 1973 image, showgirls at the Las Vegas Flamingo Hilton are a blur as they perform a number called "Fancy That." (Courtesy of UNLV Special Collections.)

Showgirls, one show boy, and clowns pose for a promotional photograph for the Hacienda show called *Ice Fantasy*. Showgirls had to be multitalented, learning how to dance on skates if they wanted to continue to work in Las Vegas shows, which raised the bar with every new production. (Courtesy of UNLV Special Collections.)

Sets, costumes, and choreography changed often in order to keep audience members interested. In this 1972 performance at the Aladdin, performers in futuristic costumes climb a web during a Minsky's Burlesque production number. (Courtesy of UNLV Special Collections.)

Three

Ponies, Mannequins, Bluebells, and Nudes

Dancing Dice Girls from the El Rancho Vegas pose in this iconic 1940s photograph. Dancers at this property had two-week contracts that ran for the duration of the show. At the end of the contract, nearly every dancer was re-signed. The pay was $75 week for six days, but all of the dancers worked seven days a week, for which they received an extra $12.50. That $12.50, however, was the exact amount of their room and board—all of the dancers resided in rooms at the back of the El Rancho Vegas. (Courtesy of Nancy Williams.)

Rusty Taylor Feuer poses in costume in this 1960s photograph. Her career as a showgirl happened completely by accident when she was "discovered" in an office building in Los Angeles. With no dancing experience whatsoever—but with the perfect height and body type—she was hired by Donn Arden and sent to Las Vegas. Prior to her career as a showgirl, Feuer served in the US Army. (Courtesy of Rusty Taylor Feuer.)

This showgirl costume from the 1950s is made of ruffles and a bikini with a simple embroidered design; it shows off dancer Bobbi Blair's legs. (Courtesy of UNLV Special Collections.)

Headdresses made with Swarovski crystals and feathers can weigh as much as 20 pounds. Note that earrings were often attached to the headdresses rather than directly on the ear. A showgirl had to learn how to balance a headdress during dance numbers and look graceful in the process. (Courtesy of UNLV Special Collections.)

Blue ostrich feathers cover Copa Girls on the stage of the Sands Hotel's Copa Room. Several types of feathers are used in showgirl costumes, including goose, pheasant, rhea, and even vulture. Feathers are twisted to make them fluffy, and each type of feather has a quality of its own, providing costume designers with the ability to create an array of different looks. (Courtesy of UNLV Special Collections.)

Copa Girls goof around while dressed in their cowgirl outfits. (Courtesy of Virginia James.)

In this August 1986 photograph, Bo Ramos, the shortest boy dancer in the Tropicana's *Folies Bergere*, stands on a chair as Sonja Lubbers, who stood a bit over six feet and two inches, adjusts his tie. (Courtesy of UNLV Special Collections.)

This 1958 photograph shows Bluebell dancers Susan Cartwright (left), Penny Parfitt (center), and Valda Boyne dressed to perform in the *C'est Magnifique* edition of the *Lido de Paris* at the Stardust. (Courtesy of UNLV Special Collections.)

Harold Minsky (left, with pipe) and an unidentified man are pictured backstage with showgirls. The beaded costumes are a precursor to the more elaborate, rhinestone-encrusted designs that would eventually become the standard uniform of Las Vegas showgirls. (Courtesy of UNLV Special Collections.)

Bras designed with rhinestones are often worn by "covered wagons," the nickname given to dancers who do not appear topless on stage. For the less-endowed women, there was a saying: "What God has forgotten, we stuff with cotton." (Courtesy of UNLV Special Collections.)

Proper application of makeup was just as important as the design of the costumes. Novice dancers often had to receive a lesson in how to apply their makeup. Features had to be well defined and exaggerated. False eyelashes were typically three layers thick, eyebrows were darkened, and lips were penciled in and covered with the only acceptable color—red. Former showgirl Betty Bunch, author of *High Heels and Headdresses*, recalls that showgirls were easily recognized due to their heavy makeup and tall stature and were thus readily admitted to nightclubs after their own shows were over. (Courtesy of UNLV Special Collections.)

Virginia James, one of the original Texas Copa Girls who came to Las Vegas to dance in shows produced by Jack Entratter, is shorter than a typical showgirl. Dancers who stood under five feet and five inches were called "ponies." (Courtesy of Virginia James.)

In this image, Harold Minsky is surrounded by showgirls. Minsky was known to be very protective of his girls, as were many of the show producers and entertainment directors. Part of the showgirls' jobs required that they mingle with casino guests after the show was over. If a guest got too familiar, however, the boss would step in and put a halt to it. Rusty Taylor Feuer recalls one man ogling her when Sands manager Carl Cohen "whip[ped] her around" and away from the offender. (Courtesy of UNLV Special Collections.)

Asian showgirls were not often seen in Las Vegas. In the image at right, Michi Otomi wears an interesting costume for the *Minsky Follies*. Fur and feathers enhance the flexible form of the piece, which is worn over a lace bodysuit. (Courtesy of UNLV Special Collections.)

Showgirls and male dancers pose with jazz great and bandleader extraordinaire Lionel Hampton (far left) at the Moulin Rouge in 1955. (Courtesy of UNLV Special Collections.)

When "nudes" (topless showgirls) initially appeared on Las Vegas stages, an uproar from the community ensued but did little to halt the spread of the trend. Many, including the showgirls themselves, saw the practice as a form of art. Here, a dancer gives the illusion of being completely naked, but she is wearing a flesh-colored G-string—a costume requirement for all dancers, regardless of whether or not they are nudes. (Courtesy of UNLV Special Collections.)

Sometimes designers found, through trial and error, that certain costumes did not work. The heavy material used for this costume made it difficult for a performer to move smoothly on stage. Its weight got heavier and heavier as the number progressed. When the curtain closed, girls in these outfits often sank to the floor and literally crawled off stage. (Courtesy of Rusty Taylor Feuer.)

This dancer is unrecognizable with beads veiling her face. The costumes worn by showgirls were a form of art designed to work with the movement of the body and enhanced by stage lighting. These creations, whether elaborately or simply designed, often stole the show. (Courtesy of UNLV Special Collections.)

These *Hallelujah Hollywood* showgirls are in costume for a number called "Sahara Madame Goes to Hollywood." The number did not require much dancing, as the headdresses were heavy and awkward. Instead, the performer's role involved movements and a lot of posing. (Courtesy of Doll-E Eaglin.)

The glory of the showgirl is apparent in the Thunderbird Hotel's production of *C'est la Femme*. (Courtesy of UNLV Special Collections.)

In the image at right, Jack Entratter chats with two showgirls during a dress rehearsal. (Courtesy of UNLV Special Collections.)

Moulin Rouge showgirls appear atop a float in 1955. (Courtesy of UNLV Special Collections.)

A nearly-nude showgirl practices her performance with an impressive headdress and little else. G-strings are often unnoticeable; the one on this costume, however, is decorated to be seen. According to Gale Baker's book, *Neon Queens*, early G-strings were called "bicycle clips" because they could attach to a girl's body without the use of elastic. (Courtesy of UNLV Special Collections.)

During the Helldorado Parade, showgirls are "arrested" and "jailed." The money spent to bail them out was used to support a good cause. It looks like "incarceration" agrees with these showgirls from the El Rancho Vegas. (Courtesy of Nancy Williams.)

These Copa Girls helped to raise money for the Las Vegas Policeman's Ball. (Courtesy of Virginia James.)

In the image at right, a little girl removes her sunglasses to get a better look at two showgirls. Perhaps, if she grows tall enough, she will follow in their footsteps. In an interview, one showgirl described how watching her mother on stage when she was a child was the inspiration for her own career as a showgirl. Although dancing had not been her lifelong dream, when she compared the $3 an hour she would make at a fast-food restaurant to the money she could earn as a showgirl, her career choice was made. (Courtesy of UNLV Special Collections.)

A showgirl's life is full of hard work and long hours, but there are many perks, such as mixing with celebrities. These showgirls from the Riviera show, *Splash*, pose with actor Burt Reynolds (center), the Riviera's entertainment director (right), and the late comedian Joey Villa. (Courtesy of Suzan Hiett Rawlings.)

In this 1977 image, Siegfried Fischbacher—of the famous Las Vegas duo Siegfried and Roy—celebrates his birthday with showgirls and other friends. (Courtesy of Ingrid Gates Jackson.)

Frank Sinatra, in costume, enjoys a moment with one of the Sands Copa Girls. (Courtesy of Virginia James.)

Virginia James poses with Jack Benny, who helped her secure a Hollywood screen test. A chance to work in Hollywood films was not uncommon for Las Vegas showgirls; their beauty was their calling card. (Courtesy of Virginia James.)

Actor and comedian Wally Cox introduces showgirls competing in one of the many contests to find the Las Vegas "Showgirl of the Year." (Courtesy of Bo Boisvert.)

Red Skelton, who performed as a headliner at the Sands in the 1960s, takes a picture of two beauties dressed in elegant costumes. (Courtesy of UNLV Special Collections.)

Her body framed with feathers and minimal material, a showgirl poses backstage as a technician prepares to give her a microphone. Pasties cover her breasts, indicating that this photograph was taken before the advent of the topless showgirl, introduced by Harold Minsky in the late 1950s. (Courtesy of Frank Valeri.)

Michael St. John (center), a columnist who wrote for *Inside Gossip* and *Now Magazine* in the 1970s, covered the story of MGM Grand introducing black showgirls. Called the Black Corps or Group C, these showgirls danced in *Hallelujah Hollywood*. When asked why no white showgirls were allowed to dance with them during the early years of the show, Doll-E Eaglin recalled that the entertainment director at the time said the mix would be "too distracting." (Courtesy of Ingrid Gates Jackson.)

A Moulin Rouge showgirl poses poolside in this 1955 photograph. (Courtesy of UNLV Special Collections.)

Suzan Hiett, a showgirl in productions such as *Playboy's Girls of Rock & Roll* and *Splash*, participates in Bring Your Child to Work Day—showgirl-style—as she walks her son across the stage to help a Las Vegas audience bring in the New Year. (Courtesy of Suzan Hiett Rawlings.)

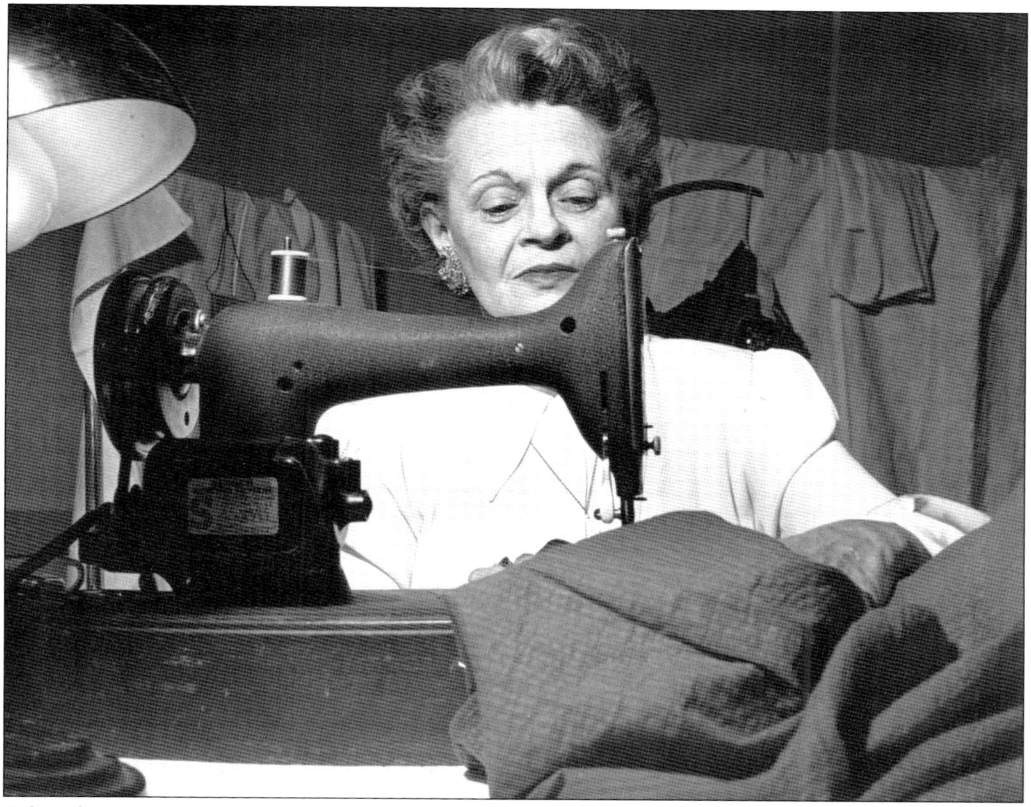

After the company manager, the showgirl's best friend is the wardrobe manager. It behooves showgirls to take extra care with their costumes, which is not easy when rhinestones and jewelry get caught in stockings and costume materials. To repair fishnets, a seamstress uses material from stockings that are beyond repair. Ripped costumes are another matter; repairs on these can be costly and difficult, especially when replacement materials are no longer available. The seamstress pictured above and at right is named Pauline (her last name is lost to history), and she worked at the Sands in the 1950s and/or 1960s. (Courtesy of UNLV Special Collections.)

A showgirl gets a quick fix to her stockings before she has to return to the stage. (Courtesy of UNLV Special Collections.)

Bluebell Valda Boyne (seated) confers with Enid Mills backstage in front of a cluttered dressing table. (Courtesy of UNLV Special Collections.)

A dancer poses next to drawers brimming with the accoutrements included in a showgirl's onstage wardrobe. (Courtesy of UNLV Special Collections.)

Sands show producer Jack Entratter serves as the number "1" as he and six Copa Girls portray the figure of "$1,000,000." The dollar amount represents the salaries Entratter had paid to 4,215 Copa Girls since he made the Copacabana label famous in the 1940s. Entratter brought the Copa Girls to Las Vegas and the Sands Hotel in the 1950s. (Courtesy of UNLV Special Collections.)

Former mayor of Las Vegas Oscar Goodman never made a public appearance without showgirls as his escorts. Claiming to be the "happiest mayor in America," Goodman did much to promote his beloved city and the characteristics that make it unique. (Courtesy of Lisa Gioia-Acres.)

This is a postcard captures an early version of the Las Vegas showgirl. (Courtesy of Phil Jensen.)

Ffolliott Charlton was a showgirl before changing her name and becoming known as the incomparable Fluff LeCoque. After serving as producer Donn Arden's second-in-command for years, she became company manager for the Bally's show, *Jubilee!*, until her retirement after 30 years with the show. Showgirls who worked under LeCoque have high praise for the woman whose career spanned the entire history of showgirls in Las Vegas. (Courtesy of UNLV Special Collections.)

A showgirl from *Minsky Follies* leans on a light post against a French-themed backdrop. (Courtesy of UNLV Special Collections.)

A Minsky showgirl strikes a seductive pose in a costume made of shimmering black material and rhinestones. (Courtesy of UNLV Special Collections.)

This showgirl is sporting a costume of black and white raffia and a headdress made with what appear to be ostrich feathers. The costume offers quite a lot of coverage—unusual for showgirl attire. (Courtesy of UNLV Special Collections.)

A backpack provides the structure for this costume. A frame made of steel and wire is what adds weight to a costume consisting mostly of feathers. (Courtesy of UNLV Special Collections.)

These showgirls entice hungry patrons to visit the Stardust's dining room. (Courtesy of UNLV Special Collections.)

A showgirl demonstrates her flexibility atop a diving board at the Sands. (Courtesy of UNLV Special Collections.)

From the feathered headdress to the perfectly tailored costume that highlights her legs, this showgirl displays confidence and style. (Courtesy of UNLV Special Collections.)

Show producers and company managers were able to assess the performers when they posed for photographs in costume, gauging to see if a dancer's weight had changed or if tan lines showed, both of which were often a basis for suspension. (Courtesy of UNLV Special Collections.)

With the arrival of productions and showgirls from Europe, feathers began to make an appearance on Vegas showgirls' costumes, as shown here. (Courtesy of UNLV Special Collections.)

A Marie Antoinette–inspired look showcases the best attributes of this stunning showgirl. The width of the skirt enhances the bodice, neckline, and choker. Along with her perfect posture, this showgirl has a swanlike appearance. (Courtesy of UNLV Special Collections.)

"A pretty girl is like a melody that haunts you night and day"—lyrics taken from a song in the 1936 MGM movie *The Great Ziegfeld*—accompanied this showgirl when she made her way across the stage. Adorned in artfully draped rhinestones, she is the image of a goddess. (Courtesy of Ingrid Gates Jackson.)

In this 1975 image, a dancer poses in an Egyptian scene from the *Casino de Paris* show at the Dunes. (Courtesy of UNLV Special Collections.)

A group of Copa Girls stands on podiums after winning first, second, and third place in a contest. The winner is in the center. (Courtesy of UNLV Special Collections.)

This beautifully crafted costume frames this showgirl's long legs. Her hat, designed with cutout flowers, sits precariously upon her head. (Courtesy of UNLV Special Collections.)

In this 1977 image, a showgirl from the Tropicana's *Folies Bergere* strikes a playful pose in this explosion of feathers dubbed the "Toilet Bowl." Costumes often acquired nicknames, including "Mae West," "Baby Huey," "Mount Vesuvius," and the "747." (Courtesy of UNLV Special Collections.)

Donning a beautifully detailed costume complete with opera gloves and sparkling jewelry made the wearer feel, as one showgirl put it, "gorgeous and proud." (Courtesy of UNLV Special Collections.)

According to dancer Ingrid Gates, this number had Black Corps dancers dressed as servants for a scene in the MGM Grand production *Hallelujah Hollywood*. (Courtesy of Ingrid Gates Jackson.)

A June Taylor Dancer poses on tiptoe. June Taylor Dancers performed at the El Rancho Vegas and other Las Vegas Strip resorts. (Courtesy of UNLV Special Collections.)

Nancy Williams poses for the camera. Williams began dancing at the El Rancho Vegas in 1948 and retired in 1956 to open a dance studio. An expert seamstress, Williams now owns and operates Williams Costumes Company, a 30-year-old business in downtown Las Vegas. (Courtesy of Nancy Williams.)

A costume made out of balloons covers this showgirl in all the right places. (Courtesy of Frank Valeri.)

A Minsky showgirl looks perfectly dainty in this pixie/ballerina costume. (Courtesy of UNLV Special Collections.)

Wings of feathers, a fur cape, and artfully draped beads lend a sunburst effect to this showgirl and her costume. (Courtesy of UNLV Special Collections.)

This showgirl, who is veiled from head to toe, embodies illusion, inaccessibility, and a hint of seduction. (Courtesy of UNLV Special Collections.)

The outrageously tall headpiece worn by this dancer delivers an imposing image, perpetuating the statuesque, goddess-like archetype of the showgirl. (Courtesy of Rusty Taylor Feuer.)

Twin showgirls were a rarity, and identical twins such as these two must have garnered a lot of attention. Although the twins pictured below are unidentified, Joan and Jane Ryba, well-known twin showgirls, appeared together at the Sands and the Desert Inn. (Courtesy of UNLV Special Collections.)

Feathers, flesh, and fishnets—along with sparkling costume jewelry—constitute the standard outfit of the Las Vegas showgirl. (Courtesy of UNLV Special Collections.)

In this photograph, it is readily apparent how Swarovski crystals and stage lighting are used to awe the audience. (Courtesy of Doll-E Eaglin.)

A showgirl embodies beauty and grace. This flowing costume is made to work with a dancer's movements to provide an elegant visual experience. (Courtesy of UNLV Special Collections.)

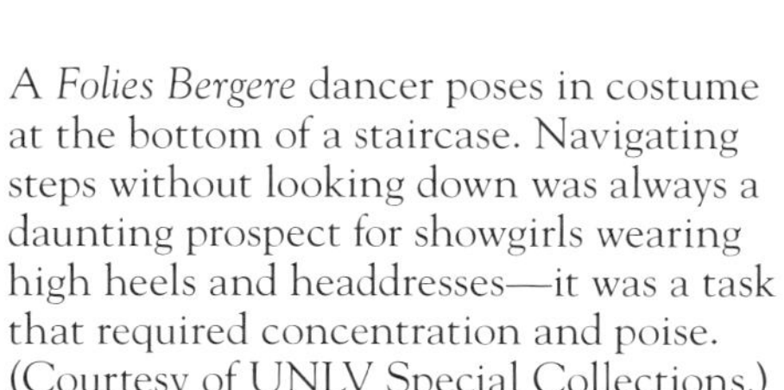

A *Folies Bergere* dancer poses in costume at the bottom of a staircase. Navigating steps without looking down was always a daunting prospect for showgirls wearing high heels and headdresses—it was a task that required concentration and poise. (Courtesy of UNLV Special Collections.)

A topless Minsky showgirl is ensconced in an intriguing, curious costume. She poses in what is likely the only stance possible in this narrow-bottomed creation. (Courtesy of UNLV Special Collections.)

Tight-fitting costumes, such as the one worn by this showgirl, required small steps on stage. Many showgirls were classically trained dancers, yet they had to learn a whole new set of skills in order to maneuver in the elaborate costumes created for Las Vegas productions. (Courtesy of UNLV Special Collections.)

A *Lido de Paris* showgirl poses in this 1988 publicity photograph. (Courtesy of UNLV Special Collections.)

Two dancers playfully pose with a bat for a sports-themed dance number at the Desert Inn. (Courtesy of Rusty Taylor Feuer.)

Fruit adorns this topless showgirl dressed for an unknown production number. (Courtesy of UNLV Special Collections.)

Sands showgirls primp in their dressing room between dances. (Courtesy of UNLV Special Collections.)

Sands showgirl Tina Olsen wears a simple yet stunning outfit adorned with large sequins. (Courtesy of UNLV Special Collections.)

Appearing to be nude is part of the allure of the showgirl; this ballerina must have looked amazing as she glided across the stage in her sheer outfit. (Courtesy of UNLV Special Collections.)

Dancers at the Flamingo Hilton form a high-kick line and keep in perfect sync with one another in this 1973 photograph of a number called "Fancy That." (Courtesy of UNLV Special Collections.)

Fur, feathers, and a shimmering dress provide a glimpse of the glamour of the early Las Vegas show days. (Courtesy of Bo Boisvert.)

From the look of her headdress, this showgirl may have been part of a number involving space aliens. (Courtesy of UNLV Special Collections.)

Copa Girls mug for the camera in a dressing room at the Sands. (Courtesy of Virginia James.)

Two dancers hide behind a lead performer as they represent a six-armed Hindu goddess. (Courtesy of UNLV Special Collections.)

A swarm of statuesque showgirls waits for a signal to return to the stage to perform in the *Lido de Paris* show at the Stardust. (Courtesy of Suzan Hiett Rawlings.)

This 1988 photograph shows *Lido de Paris* dancers. The show debuted at the Stardust on July 2, 1958. (Courtesy of UNLV Special Collections.)

The perfect showgirl pose is demonstrated here: the raised arm, the impeccable posture, and the enduring smile. (Courtesy of UNLV Special Collections.)

Costumes were beginning to push the envelope when this picture was taken of Last Frontier dancers showing their bellybuttons for the very first time. Note that the midriff is still covered by sheer netting. (Courtesy of Nancy Williams.)

"Mannequin" is a nickname often used to describe showgirls, who are seen by some as mediums for displaying costume creations. This photograph shows Doll-E Eaglin posing as a "mannequin" from *Hallelujah Hollywood.* Other nicknames categorized dancers based on their body types ("short" or "tall") or their costumes ("nude" or "covered"). (Courtesy of Doll-E Eaglin.)

Vive les Girls ran at the Dunes from 1961 through the 1970s. This *Vive les Girls* performer personifies the playful and glamorous character of the Las Vegas showgirl, an icon who helped to fashion the enduring enticement of a city visited by millions of tourists who hope to experience a bit of the magic that is Las Vegas. Viva les Showgirls! (Courtesy of UNLV Special Collections.)

Bibliography

Baker, Gale. *Neon Queens*. Auburn, CA: eBookstand Books, 1999.
Bunch, Betty. *High Heels and Headdresses: Memoirs of a Vintage Vegas Showgirl*. Stephens Press, 2011.
Las Vegas Review-Journal
Medford, Lisa, and Jeanne Gulbranson. *I Can Hear the Applause: Adult Language . . . Some Nudity*. Emperor Penguin Publishing, 2010.
Unknown author. "But Dad, It's ONLY a Job." *Las Vegas Sun*. March 19, 1980.

Consistent with our mission to preserve history on a local level, this book was printed in South Carolina on American-made paper and manufactured entirely in the United States. Products carrying the accredited Forest Stewardship Council (FSC) label are printed on 100 percent FSC-certified paper.